W9-ANK-991

BOOKS BY JAMES MERRILL

POETRY

The Fire Screen   1969
Nights and Days   1966
Water Street   1962
The Country of a Thousand Years of Peace   1959
First Poems   1951

FICTION

The (Diblos) Notebook   1965
The Seraglio   1957

THE FIRE SCREEN

THE FIRE SCREEN

POEMS BY

JAMES MERRILL

ATHENEUM   NEW YORK   1969

Last Words and *The Summer People* first appeared in THE
ATLANTIC MONTHLY; *The Friend of the Fourth Decade* and *Words
for Maria*, in THE NEW YORKER; *Pola Diva* and *Matinees*, in
POETRY. Other poems are reprinted by courtesy of THE BROWN
BAG, THE HUDSON REVIEW, IMPRESSIONS WORKSHOP, THE
MASSACHUSETTS REVIEW, THE NATION, THE NEW REPUBLIC, THE
NEW YORK REVIEW OF BOOKS, NORTHWEST REVIEW, PARTISAN
REVIEW, QUARTERLY REVIEW OF LITERATURE, SALMAGUNDI,
SHENANDOAH, and THE STEPPENWOLF.

Published simultaneously in Canada by McClelland and Stewart Ltd
Library of Congress catalog number 71–86549
Composed and printed by Clarke & Way, New York
Bound by H. Wolff, New York
Designed by Harry Ford
First Edition

FOR DAVID JACKSON

CONTENTS

THE FIRE SCREEN

LORELEI

The stones of kin and friend
Stretch off into a trembling, sweatlike haze.

They may not after all be stepping-stones
But you have followed them. Each strands you, then

Does not. Not yet. Not here.
Is it a crossing? Is there no way back?

Soft gleams lap the base of the one behind you
On which a black girl sings and combs her hair.

It's she who some day (when your stone is in place)
Will see that much further into the golden vagueness

Forever about to clear. Love with his chisel
Deepens the lines begun upon your face.

THE FRIEND OF THE FOURTH DECADE

When I returned with drinks and nuts my friend
Had moved to the window seat, back to the view.

The clear central pane around which ran
Smaller ones stained yellow, crimson, blue,

Framed our country's madly whipping flag,
Its white pole above roofs, the sea beyond.

That it was time for the flag to be lowered shed
Light on my friend's tactful disinvolvement—

Or did he feel as chastening somehow
Those angry little stripes upon his shoulders?

A huge red sun flowed positively through
Him in spots, glazing, obscuring his person

To that of Anyman with ears aglow,
On a black cushion, gazing inward, mute.

After dinner he said, "I'm tired of understanding
The light in people's eyes, the smells, the food.

(By the way, those veal birds were delicious.
They're out of Fannie Farmer? I thought so.)

Tired of understanding what I hear,
The tones, the overtones; of knowing

Just what clammy twitchings thrive
Under such cold flat stones

As We-are-profoundly-honored-to-have-with-us
Or This-street-has-been-torn-up-for-your-convenience.

As for what I catch myself saying,
Don't believe me! I *despise* Thoreau.

I mean to learn, in the language of where I am going,
Barely enough to ask for food and love.

Listen," he went on. "I have this friend—
What's that face for? Did you think I had only one?

You are my oldest friend, remember. Well:
Karlheinrich collects stamps. I now spend mornings

With a bowl of water and my postcard box.
Cards from all over. God! Those were the years

I never used to throw out anything.
Each card then soaks five minutes while its ink

Turns to exactly the slow formal swirls
Through which a phoenix flies on Chinese silk.

These leave the water darker but still clear,
The text unreadable. It's true!

Cards from my mother, my great-uncle, you!
And the used waters deepen the sea's blue.

I cannot tell you what this does to me.
Scene upon scene's immersion and emergence

Rinsed of the word. The Golden Gate, Moroccan
Dancing boys, the Alps from Interlaken,

Fuji, the Andes, Titian's Venus, two
Mandrills from the Cincinnati zoo—

All *that* survives the flood, as does a lighter
Heart than I have had in many a day.

Salt lick big as a fist, heart, hoard
Of self one grew up prizing above rubies—

To feel it even by a grain dissolved,
Absolved I mean, recipient with writer,

By water holy from the tap, by air that dries,
Of having cared and having ceased to care . . ."

I nodded and listened, envious. When my friend
Had gone where he was going, I tried it, too.

The stamp slid off, of course, and the ink woke.
I watched my mother's *Dearest Son* unfurl

In blue ornate brief plungings-up:
Almost a wild iris taking shape.

I heard oblivion's thin siren singing,
And bore it bravely. At the hour's end

I had my answer. Chances are it was
Some simple matter of what ink she used,

And yet her message remained legible,
The memories it stirred did not elude me.

I put my postcards back upon the shelf.
Certain things die only with oneself.

"You should see Muhammed's taxi," wrote my friend.
"Pure junkyard Bauhaus, angular, dented white,

It trails a wedding veil of squawking dust.
Each ride is worth your life—except I'm just

Not afraid. I'm not.
Those chiefly who discern us have the juju

To take our lives. Bouncing beside Muhammed,
I smile and smoke, am indestructible.

Or else I just can't picture dying
On foreign soil. These years are years of grace.

The way I feel towards home is . . . dim.
Don't worry, I'll go back. Honeymoons end.

Nor does the just man cheat his native earth
Of its inalienable right to cover him."

Finally a dung-and-emerald oasis,
No place I knew of. "Here," he wrote on the back,

"Individual and type are one.
Do as I please, I *am* the simpleton

Whose last exploit is to have been exploited
Neck and crop. In the usual bazaar,

Darker, more crisscrossed than a beggar's palm,
Smell of money draws them after me,

I answer to whatever name they call,
Drink the sweet black condescending dregs,

Try on their hungers like a shirt of flame
(Well, a sports shirt of flame) whereby I've been

Picked clean, reborn each day increasingly
Conspicuous, increasingly unseen."

Behind a door marked DANGER
(This is a dream I have about my friend)

Swaddlings of his whole civilization,
Prayers, accounts, long priceless scroll,

Whip, hawk, prow, queen, down to some last
Lost comedy, all that fine writing

Rigid with rains and suns,
Are being gingerly unwound.

There. Now the mirror. Feel the patient's heart
Pounding—oh please, this once—

Till nothing moves but to a drum.
See his eyes darken in bewilderment—

No, in joy—and his lips part
To greet the perfect stranger.

16.IX.65

for Vassili and Mimi

Summer's last half moon waning high
Dims and curdles. Up before the bees
On our friend's birthday, we have left him
To wake in their floating maze.

Light downward strokes of yellow, green, and rust
Render the almond grove. Trunk after trunk
Tries to get right, in charcoal,
The donkey's artless contrapposto.

Sunrise. On the beach
Two turkey gentlemen, heads shaven blue
Above dry silk kimonos sashed with swords,
Treat us to a Kabuki interlude.

The tiny fish risen excitedly
Through absolute transparence
Lie in the boat, gasping and fanning themselves
As if the day were warmer than the sea.

Cut up for bait, our deadest ones
Reappear live, by magic, on the hook.
Never anything big or gaudy—
Line after spangled line of light, light verse.

A radio is playing "Mack the Knife".
The morning's catch fills one straw hat.
Years since I'd fished. Who knows when in this life
Another chance will come?

Between our toes unused to sandals
Each step home strikes its match.
And now, with evenings four and twenty candles
Lit among stars, waves, pines

To animate our friend's face, all our faces
About a round, sweet loaf,
Mavríli brays. We take him some,
Return with honey on our drunken feet.

WORDS FOR MARIA

Unjeweled in black as ever comedienne
Of mourning if not silent star of chic,
You drift, September nightwind at your back,
The half block from your flat to the Bon Goût,
Collapse, order a black
Espresso and my ouzo in that Greek
Reserved for waiters, crane to see who's who
Without removing your dark glasses, then,
Too audibly: "Eh, Jimmy, qui sont ces deux strange men?"

Curiosity long since killed the cat
Inside you. Sweet good nature, lack of guile,
These are your self-admitted foibles, no?
My countrymen, the pair in question, get
Up, glance our way, and go,
And we agree it will not be worthwhile
To think of funny nicknames for them yet,
Such as Le Turc, The Missing Diplomat,
Justine, The Nun, The Nut—ah now, speaking of that,

I'm calling *you* henceforth The Lunatic.
Today at 4 a.m. in a snack bar
You were discovered eating, if you please,
Fried squid; alone. Aleko stood aghast.
"Sit down, try some of these,"
You said and gave your shrug, as when, the car
Door shutting on your thumb, a faint sigh passed
Uninterpreted till Frederick
At table glimpsed your bloodstained Kleenex and was sick.

Sapphó has been to your new flat, she *says*.
Tony, who staggered there with the Empire
Mirror you wanted from his shop, tells how
You had him prop it in a chair and leave
That instant. Really now!

Let's plan a tiny housewarming. "My dear,
Impossible with L'Eternel Convive."
Tall, gleaming, it could sit for years, I guess,
Drinking the cool black teas of your appearances.

Not that you're much at home this season. By
Ten you are being driven to the shore—
A madness known as Maria's Gardening Phase.
I went along once, watched you prune, transplant,
Nails ragged, in a daze
Of bliss. A whitewashed cube with tout confort
You'd built but would not furnish. "Bah, one can't
Spend day and night in Eden. Chairs, beds—why?
Dormir, d'ailleurs, this far from the Bon Goût? I'd die!"

In smarter weeds than Eve's (Chanel, last year's)
You kneel to beds of color and young vines.
The chauffeur lounges smoking in the shade . . .
Before you know it, sunset. Brass-white, pink-
Blue wallowings. Dismayed
You recollect a world in which one dines,
Plays cards, endures old ladies, has to think.
The motor roars. You've locked up trowel and shears.
The whole revived small headland lurches, disappears

To float pale black all night against the sea,
A past your jasmines for the present grow
Dizzyingly from. About what went before
Or lies beneath, how little one can glean.
Girlhood, marriage, the war . . .
I'd like once (not now, here comes Giulio)
Really to hear—I mean—I didn't mean—
You paint a smiling mouth to answer me:
"Since when does L'Enfant care for archaeology?"

13

"Some people are not charmed. I'm among those,"
Sapphó said, livid. "Fond of one? Pure myth.
Fond of her chauffeur—period. I refuse
Flatly to see her." As for me, I've come
To take you for the muse
Of my off-days, and tell you so herewith
If only to make you smile, shrug, run a comb
Through foam-grayed hair the wind from Egypt blows
Across a brow of faint lines powdered tuberose.

MORE ENTERPRISE

A sideways flicker, half headshake of doubt—
Meaning, confusingly, assent—fills out
The scant wardrobe of gesture I still use.
It clings by habit now. The old strait swank
I came in struts the town on local heirs.
Koula's nephew has the suit she shrank,
Andreas coveted my Roman shoes. . . .
Into the grave I'll wear that Yes of theirs.

KOSTAS TYMPAKIANAKIS

Sit, friend. We'll be drinking and I'll tell you why.
Today I went to Customs to identify
My brother—it was him, all right, in spite of both
Feet missing from beneath his Army overcoat.

He was a handsome devil twice the size of me.
We're all good-looking in my family.
If you saw that brother, or what's left of him,
You'd understand at once the kind of man he'd been.

I have other brothers, one whose face I broke
In a family quarrel, and that's no joke:
I'm small but strong, when I get mad I fight.
Seven hundred vines of his were mine by right

And still are—fine! He's welcome to them.
I'm twenty-two. It's someone else's turn to dream.
I liked our school and teacher till they made me stop
And earn my living in a welder's shop.

Cousins and friends were learning jokes and games
At the Kafeneíon behind steamed-up panes.
I worked without a mask in a cold rain of sparks
That fell on you and burned—look, you can still see marks.

The German officer stubbed his *puro* out
On my mother's nipples but her mouth stayed shut.
She lived to bear me with one foot in the grave
And they never found my father in his mountain cave.

He died last year at eighty. To his funeral
Came a NATO Captain and an English General.
Our name is known around Herakleion
In all the hill towns, just ask anyone.

Outside our village up above Knossós
A railed-in plot of cypresses belongs to us,
Where we'll put my brother, and if there's room
One day I'll lie beside him till the crack of doom.

But I'd rather travel to a far-off land,
Though I never shall, and settle, do you understand?
The trouble here is not with sun and soil
So much as meanness in the human soul.

I worked a time in Germany, I saw a whore
Smile at me from inside her little lighted door.
She didn't want my money, she was kind and clean
With mirrors we submerged in like a submarine.

The girl I loved left me for a Rhodiot.
I should be broken-hearted but it's strange, I'm not.
Take me with you when you sail next week,
You'll see a different cosmos through the eyes of a Greek.

Or write my story down for people. Use my name.
And may it bring you all the wealth and fame
It hasn't brought its bearer. Here, let's drink our wine!
Who could have imagined such a life as mine?

OUZO FOR ROBIN

Dread of an impending umptieth
Birthday thinning blood to water, clear
Spirits to this opal-tinted white—
Uncle, the confusion unto death!

Last night's hurled glass. On the wall a mark
Explored by sunlight inching blindly
Forth from the tavern onto tree-tarred
Heights of gilt and moleskin, now gone dark.

Thorn needle launched in spinning grooves' loud
Black. A salt spray, a drenching music.
Each dance done, wet hawklike features cling
To one more tumblerful of numb cloud.

Joy as part of dread, rancor as part.
Lamplit swaying rafters. Later, stars.
Case presented, point by brilliant point,
Against the uncounselable heart.

Ground trampled hard. Again. The treasure
Buried. Rancor. Joy. Tonight's blank grin.
Threshold where the woken cherub shrieks
To stop it, stamping with displeasure.

TO MY GREEK

Dear nut
Uncrackable by nuance or debate,
Eat with your fingers, wear your bloomers to bed,

Under my skin stay nude. Let past and future

Perish upon our lips, ocean inherit
Those paper millions. Let there be no word
For justice, grief, convention; *you* be convention—
Goods, bads, kaló-kakó, cockatoo-raucous

Coastline of white printless coves

Already strewn with offbeat echolalia.
Forbidden Salt Kiss Wardrobe Foot Cloud Peach
—Name it, my chin drips sugar. Radiant dumbbell, each

Noon's menus and smalltalk leave you

Likelier, each sunset yawned away,
Hair in eyes, head bent above the strummed
Lexicon, gets by heart about to fail
This or that novel mode of being together

Without conjunctions. Still

I fear for us. Nights fall
We toss through blindly, drenched in her appraising
Glare, the sibyl I turn to

When all else fails me, when you do—

The mother tongue!
Her least slip a mirror triptych glosses,
Her automation and my mind are one.
Ancient in fishscale silver-blue,

What can she make of you? Her cocktail sweats

With reason: speech will rise from it,
Quite beyond your comprehension rise
Like blood to a slapped face, stingingly apt

If unrepeatable, tones one forgets

Even as one is changed for life by them,
Veins branching a cold coral,
Common sense veering into common scenes,
Tears, incoherent artifice,

Altar upset, cut glass and opaline

Schools ricocheting through the loud cave
Where lie my Latin's rusted treasure,
The bones, picked clean, of my Italian,

Where some blue morning also she may damn

Well find her windpipe slit with that same rainbow
Edge a mere weekend with you gives
To books, to living (anything to forego
That final drunken prophecy whereby,

Lacking her blessing, you my siren grow

Stout, serviceable, gray.
A fishwife shawled in fourth-hand idiom
Spouting my views to earth and heaven)—Oh,

Having chosen the way of little knowledge,

Trusted each to use the other
Kindly except in moments of gross need,
Come put the verb-wheel down
And kiss my mouth despite the foot in it.

Let schoolboys brave her shallows. Sheer

Lilting azure float them well above
Those depths the surfacer
Lives, when he does, alone to sound and sound.

The barest word be what I say in you.

THE ENVOYS

The scurrier of the courtyard
Forth from whitewashed cranny
Behind the trumpet vine into lamplight
Frozen awaits your swooping hand.

It holds him gently, humorously.
The gullet pulses. The eye fixes on nothing.
Released, he darts from sight.
A smaller one emerges: Me! Now me!

Today you entered joyous. Not a joke.
There, patient on our very doorstep—
One moment. Had I thread?

You knotted the frail harness, spoke,
Revolved. Eureka! Round your head
Whirred a living emerald satellite.

Times, there may be some initial misunderstanding.
Phaedra, extracted from your jacket lining,
Flung herself like a bird against the glass—
Who that same night lay on your heart and purred.

The total experience depending, as it does,
Upon modulation into a brighter key
Of terror we survive to play,
I too have deeply feared.

Teach me, lizard, kitten, scarabee—
Gemmed coffer opening on the dram
Of everlasting life he represents,

His brittle pharoahs in the vale of Hence
Will hear who you are, who I am,
And how you bound him close and set him free.

"LIGHT OF THE STREET,
DARKNESS OF YOUR OWN HOUSE"

Fused wires of wit, benighted attic
Whose owl, by day unseeing, glares
Down now into haloed vacancy
There precisely where the street has given

Way to some original crooked and narrow
Cascade of refuse, cactus, rock
The struggler upward must negotiate

To get beyond those final hovels clustered
Beneath their final bulb condemned
To hang revealing *nothing* till daybreak
When it can lose itself in you,

You woken smoking, reds and greens, godsped

Along a six-lane boulevard's hard ease,
Sun of my life in your dumb horses' power
Shining drunk, the siren, the migraine,
Pigeon-throat stains, fleet bodies, love oh love—

The street, if it ends at all, ends here.
This figure watching falls asleep,
On hands and knees continues the ascent

Into ignorance forever steeper
Hooting starless until a twitch of limbs
Betrays your lodging I am dreaming yet
From the windows, from the yawning door

Beams of the first unquenchable luster pour.

...shrinking to enter, did. Your heart
Was large—you'd often told me—large but light,
Ant palace, tubercular coral sponge amazed
With passages, quite weightless in your breast.
(Or did my entrance weigh? You never said.)
In sunlit outer galleries I pondered
Names, dates, political slogans, lyrics,
Football scores, obscenities too, scrawled
Everywhere dense as lace. How alike we were!
More than pleased, I penetrated further.
Strung haphazard now through the red gloom
Were little, doorless, crudely lighted chambers:
Four waxen giants at supper; the late king;
A dust-furred dog; a whore mottled with cold,
Legs in air; your motorbike; a friend,
Glass raised despite the bandage round his head,
His eyes' false shine. What had happened to them all?
Yet other cells appeared empty but lit,
Or darkly, unimaginably tenanted.
From one, a word sobbed over, "Waste...the waste..."
Where was the terrace, the transparency
So striking far away? In my fall I struck
An iron surface (so! your heart was heavy)
Hot through clothing. Snatched myself erect.
Beneath, great valves were gasping, wheezing. What
If all you knew of me were down there, leaking
Fluids at once abubble, pierced by fierce
Impulsions of unfeeling, life, limb turning
To burning cubes, to devil's dice, to ash—
What if my effigy were down there? What,
Dear god, if it were not!
If it were nowhere in your heart!
Here I turned back. Of the rest I do not speak.
Nor was your heart so cleverly constructed
I needed more than time to get outside—

Time, scorned as I scorned the waiting daylight.
Before resuming my true size, there came
A place in which one could have scratched one's name.
But what rights had I? Didn't your image,
Still unharmed, deep in my own saved skin
Blaze on? You might yet see it, see by it.
Nothing else mattered.

AN ABDICATION

First I looked at water. It was good.
Blue oblongs glinted from afar. From close
I saw it moving, hueless, clear
Down to a point past which nothing was clear
Or moving, and I had to close
My eyes. The water had done little good.

A second day I tried the trees. They stood
In a rich stupor, altogether
Rooted in the poor, the hard, the real.
But then my mind began to reel—
Elsewhere, smoother limbs would grow together.
How should the proffered apple be withstood?

One dusk upon my viewless throne
I realized the housecat's tyrant nature,
Let her features small and grave
Look past me as into their shallow grave.
No animal could keep me from a nature
Which existed to be overthrown.

Man at last, the little that I own
Is not long for this world. My cousin's eye
Lights on a rust-red, featherweight
Crown of thoughts. He seems to wait
For me to lift it from my brow (as I
Now do) and place it smartly on his own.

NIKE

The lie shone in her face before she spoke it.
Moon-battered, cloud-torn peaks, mills, multitudes
Implied. A floating sphere
Her casuist had at most to suck his pen,
Write of *Unrivalled by truth's own*
For it to dawn upon me. Near the gate
A lone iris was panting, purple-tongued.
I thought of my village, of tonight's *Nabucco*
She would attend, according to the lie,
Bemedalled at the royal right elbow. High
Already on entr'acte kümmel, hearing as always
Through her ears the sad waltz of the slaves,
I held my breath in pity for the lie
Which nobody would believe unless I did.
Mines (unexploded from the last one) lent
Drama to its rainbow surface tension.
Noon struck. Far off, a cataract's white thread
Kept measuring the slow drop into the gorge.
I thought of his forge and crutch who hobbled
At her prayer earthward. What he touched bloomed.
Fire-golds, oil-blacks. The pond people
Seemed victims rather, bobbing belly-up,
Of constitutional vulnerability
Than dynamite colluding with a fast buck.
Everywhere soldiers were falling, reassembling,
As we unpacked our picnic, she and I.
No wiser than the ant. Prepared to die
For all we knew. And even at the end,
Faced with a transcript bound in sunset
Of muffled depositions underground,
She offered wine and cookies first. She asked,
Before the eyes were bandaged, the bubble burst
And what she uttered with what I held back
Ran in red spittle down the chin,
Asked why I could not have lived the lie.

Flicking a crumb off, diffident, asked why
I thought my loved ones had been left to dream
Whole nights unbridled in the bed's brass jail
Beneath a ceiling washed by her reflected snows.

FLYING FROM BYZANTIUM

1

The hour has come. I'm heading home.
We take a cab to the airdrome
In time for the last brandy.
I've kept my Kodak handy
To snap the last unfocused Kodachrome.

Our linen's at the laundromat.
What will become of the gray cat
I'd rather not conjecture.
As for my regular lecture
—Kindness to Animals—I'll spare you that.

But a near lightning sheets the brain.
I cannot take your hand for pain.
Your brows knit above lonely
Filling eyes. If only
I thought that I would look in them again!

Crack! Mountain lurches, villas tilt,
Pale green coves right themselves unspilt
But smaller oh and faster,
Pace of the young ringmaster
Whipping to shreds of cloud a world he built.

Now to say something I'll regret—
It's not true, it's not true, and yet—
God save me from more living.
I loved you, I am leaving.
Another world awaits me? I forget.

You, you whose animal I am,
My senses' mage and pentagram,
Look, listen, miles above you
I love you still, I love you...
Then get in line to board the long slow tram.

2

Up spoke the man in the moon:
"What does that moan mean?
The plane was part of the plan.
Why gnaw the bone of a boon?"

I said with spleen, "Explain
These nights that tie me in knots,
All drama and no dream,
While you lampoon my pain."

He then: "Lusters are least
Dimmed among the damned.
The point's to live, love,
Not shake your fist at the feast.

So up from your vain divan,
The one on which you wane.
I've shown you how to shine—
Show me the moon in man!"

I rose to an old ruse,
Prepared to sell my soul
If need be. North winds neighed,
A blaze of silver blues

Flooded the scene, no sign
That either heart had been hurt.
The years shone back on yours
Free and immune from mine.

3

The priceless metal bird came down
At last. On either side were harsh
Foothills and an endless marsh.
He did not take the bus to town.

Suns rose and set in crimson dust.
Mountain lion, watersnake—
As if the choice were his to make,
Kneeling there on the earth's crust.

"Mother, I was vain, headstrong,
Help me, I am coming back."
He put his lips along a crack,
Inhaled the vague, compliant song.

"That I may be born again
Lead the black fly to my flesh."
Far off a young scribe turned a fresh
Page, hesitated, dipped his pen.

LAST WORDS

My life, your light green eyes
Have lit on me with joy.
There's nothing I don't know
Or shall not know again,
Over and over again.
It's noon, it's dawn, it's night,
I am the dog that dies
In the deep street of Troy
Tomorrow, long ago—
Part of me dims with pain,
Becomes the stinging flies,
The bent head of the boy.
Part looks into your light
And lives to tell you so.

Into the flame Godmother put her hand,
Lulling the olive boughs.
Lymph welled from them. I too in her strange house
Kindled and smoked and did not understand.

Followed the Cyclopean meal:
Loaves, rice, hens, goats, gallons of sweet red wine.
I mellowed with the men
Who now waxed crackling, philosophical

—For all I knew—but then
Were on their feet, with flashlights, tramping out
In ancient Air Force overcoats
After the small birds roosting roundabout.

Chains glowing strong
Had bound me to her hearth. Photograph time!
A whole boxful explained in pantomime,
One by one. The string

Retied, warm-hearted questioning
Could start, in mime, about my life.
Each offhand white lie gladdened her, good queen
In whose domain the rueful

Dream was fact. Subdued
Came back her hunters. The lone ortolan,
Head lolling from a sideboard out of Oudry,
Would be my very own to breakfast on.

Bedtime. Inconceivable upper room
Ashiver in lamplight.
Bed clean as ice, heavy as ice
Its layers of coarsely woven pink and white

Woken at once to struggle out from. Bitter
Closet reeking welcome. Wind, moon, frost.
Piebald hindquarters of another guest.
Fowl's nervous titter.

Relieved of wine's last warmth, to lie and freeze . . .
Day would break, never fear;
Rime-sparkling courtesies melt into blue air
Like dew. One hour more? Two? Goodbye! Write please!

The road would climb in bracelets toward the pass,
The sun be high but low,
Each olive tree shed its white thawing shadow
On sallow grass,

Myself become the stranger who remembers
Fire, cold, a smile, a smell,
One tiny plucked form on the embers,
Slow claw raised in blessing or farewell.

ANOTHER AUGUST

Pines. The white, ochre-pocked houses. Sky unflawed. Upon
so much former strangeness a calm settles, glaze of custom to
be neither shattered nor shattered by. Home. Home at last.

> Years past—blind, tattering
> wind, hail, tears—my head was in those clouds
> that now are dark pearl in my head.
>
> Open the shutters. Let variation
> abandon the swallows one by one.
> How many summer dusks were needed
> to make that single skimming form!
> The very firefly kindles to its type.
> Here is each evening's lesson. First
> the hour, the setting. Only then
> the human being, his white shirtsleeve
> chalked among treetrunks, round a waist,
> or lifted in an entrance. Look for him.
> Be him.

Envoi for S.

Whom you saw mannerless and dull of heart,
Easy to fool, impossible to hurt,
I wore that fiction like a fine white shirt
And asked no favor but to act the part.

REMORA

This life is deep and dense
Beyond all seeing, yet one sees, in spite
Of being littler, a degree or two
Further than those one is attracted to.

Pea-brained, myopic, often brutal,
When chosen they have no defense—
A sucking sore there on the belly's pewter—
And where two go could be one's finer sense.

Who now descends from a machine
Plumed with bubbles, death in his right hand?
Lunge, numbskull! One, two, three worlds boil.
Thanks for the lift. There are other fish in the sea.

Still on occasion as by oversight
One lets be taken clinging fast
In heavenly sunshine to the corpse a slight
Tormented self, live, dapper, black-and-white.

A FEVER

Two nights with her and I have caught the virus.
She leaves—for an hour? for ever? There is no knowing. I
    rouse
A chattering self. The thermometer quickly allows
It is not the least susceptible of her admirers.

Pull down the blind, crawl back to bed in gloom
Bright points keep being made through, monocle on black
Cord twirling—whose parchment dandy now with a
    merciless crack
Up and disappears. Delirium.

Where are the chimneys, the traffic? Instead come strange
Horizons of ink, and livid treetops massing raggedly
Beyond the sill like poor whites in a study
Of conditions we must one day seriously try to change.

Enter the moon like a maid in silence unsheeting the waste
Within, of giant toys, toy furniture.
Two button eyes transfix me. A voice blurred and impure,
Speaks through lips my own lips have effaced:

"Back so soon? Am I to wish you joy, as usual,
Of a new friend? For myself, not quite the nice
Young thing first given to your gentleness,
These visits are my life, which is otherwise uneventful."

I touch her snarled hair and contrive to answer:
"Dear—" but have forgotten her very name!—"dear heart,
How do you do? Speak freely, without art.
You have in me a sympathetic listener."

"I have in you nothing. Look at me. I am yours
Merely, as you've been told dozens of times already—
Though you may need reminding now that this season's lady
Deploys her pearl or coral apertures."

"You dolls who talk of broken faith," I say in fun,
"Yield to the first comer, to the twentieth."
But she: "I cannot vouch for others here on earth.
Le coeur n'est point, Seigneur, un don qui se redonne."

"Ah, so we know French? I congratulate—"
"What you know I know. That alone. No deeper thread,
Blacker, tougher, needles this soft head.
Such knowledge is its own forgiveness and my fate."

"Bravo! Asleep in a chest you kept informed of the middle-
      aged
Me who loves Verdi and Venice, who registers voters?"
"I woke always to music. A wake of waters
Dipped in brass your weakness for the underprivileged.

Look at me! How much do I sleep? Neglect and damage
Aren't dreams. Their dry dews fall. Their webs exhaust.
The point was to be one on whom nothing is lost,
But what is gained by one more random image

Crossed with mine at one more feast of crumbs?
The mirror wrinkles and wears, the drink undoes like a shirt.
Dream stain, the tears, the mendings—they all hurt;
The last, I have heard and believe, entirely consumes.

In time, in time..." Her voice dies away, singsong:
"When the mice ate my sugar heart what did you feel...?"
Now only do I look, and see the wound, and kneel
Beside her on the dream's bare boards. A long

Spell seems to pass before I am found in a daze,
Cheek touching floor. From a position so low
Colors passionate but insubstantial fill the window.
Must it begin and end like this always?

My girl has come back as promised from the seashore, young,
Blithe in some latest fashion, and her face
Freshly made up bends down to evening's deep embrace.
I savor the thin paints upon my tongue.

MORNINGS IN A NEW HOUSE

And still at dawn the fire is lit
By whom a cold man hardly cares,
Reflection gliding up the legs of chairs,
Flue choking with the shock of it.

Next a frozen window thaws
In gradual slow stains of field,
Snow fence and birches more or less revealed.
This done, the brightness sheathes its claws.

The worst is over. Now between
His person and that tamed uprush
(Which to recall alone can make him flush)
Habit arranges the fire screen.*

Crewel-work. His mother as a child
Stitched giant birds and flowery trees
To dwarf a house, *her* mother's—see the chimney's
Puff of dull yarn! Still vaguely chilled,

Guessing how even then her eight
Years had foreknown him, nursed him, all,
Sewn his first dress, sung to him, let him fall,
Howled when his face chipped like a plate,

*Days later. All framework & embroidery rather than any slower look-
ing into things. Fire screen—screen *of* fire. The Valkyrie's baffle, pulsing at trance pitch, godgiven, elemental. Flames masking that cast-iron
plaque—'contrecoeur' in French—which backs the hearth with charred
Loves & Graces. Some such meaning might have caught, only I didn't
wait, I settled for the obvious—by lamplight as it were. Oh well. Our
white heats lead us on no less than words do. Both have been devices in
their day.

40

He stands there wondering until red
Infraradiance, wave on wave,
So enters each plume-petal's crazy weave,
Each worsted brick of the homestead,

That once more, deep indoors, blood's drawn,
The tiny needlewoman cries,
And to some faintest creaking shut of eyes
His pleasure and the doll's are one.

Angrier than my now occasional
Rum-blossom, to adolescence come
Deep buds of pain. The blood-stained butcher-boy
And Laure at the clavier who would not smile
Were sufferers no less than the Sun King
Spots on whose countenance, the theory goes,
Must answer for that August
Of dry electric storms, of leaves'
Incendiary pamphlets fluttering.
History's lesson? What is young and burns,
Complexion of the boy, the star, the age,
Invites disfigurement. Too late
The shepherdess, her peach-bloom criminal,
Was recognized as queen. Too soon
The cleaver glittered and the chord was struck,
And in the dark that mercifully fell
You had arisen, gibbous moon,
Lit by such laws as exile both of us
From the eruptions of a court whose pageants
These deeply-pitted features chronicle.

THE OPERA COMPANY

1

The impresario
Consigned to the pit

Energy, mass. He was prouder
Of effects that called for

The voice like a green branch
Lifted in gales,

The fat, scaled voice aflicker
From a cleft, the soaring,

Glancing fountain-voice, the voice
Of stone that sank;

This afternoon's effulgence,
Last night's crystallizations.

Season after season, swallowtail,
Unborn seal, pearl stomacher,

We flowed through slow red vestibules
To hear the great ones in their prime and ours.

Now if, of a night, our box is empty
And Chinese students fill the impresario's,

His cosmos wheezes into bloom regardless,
The seal outwits the airhole, and the all-star casts

Of polar ice break up, shining and drowning
Unconscionably in the summer sea.

2

The rival sopranos sang on alternate evenings.
The maid of one was sent
To fumigate the prima donna's dressing room
After the other had used it—who retaliated
By praising everything about the first:
Technique, beauty, age.

From the one's throat
Spurted into darkness
Gouts of adamant, a panoramic ramp
Lit and ascended in cold blood.
Those heights attacked, she struck
One ravishing blank attitude
Against the dead composer's starry mind.

The other's eyelids shut,
An autumn-rose hallucination rippled
Over waves, inward. Rock would blush
And seed swell, yes, and rapture flaw itself.
Another season, and the very song
Had forked, had broken
Flowing into clay.

Came the inevitable war. The one
Married a copper magnate and performed
Before the enemy. The other
Opened a ranch for divorcées.

Dependably for either, every night
Tenors had sobbed their hearts out, grates
Fluttering with strips of red and orange paper.
Such fires were fiction? Then explain
These ashes, if you please.

Less and less I rake them. Of the rivals
One is old now, one dead.
And I had never heard before today
The LP on whose cover my two loves
Wonderfully smiling have linked arms.
It's of some Brahms duets cut lord knows when
And issued with regrets for low fidelity.
What is my happiness, my dismay?
Lightly the needle touches my spinning heart,
The voices soar and mix, will not be told apart.

3
After the war
No jewel remained but feeling.
The head held itself high beneath
Instinct red and branchy, torn from depths,
The bleached jaws of the serpent or the cat.
No more tiaras. Joys, humiliations,
Greed's bluewhite choker, guilt beading the brow—
Thus we arrayed
Our women, and were proud.
The actual stones were kept or not, like Bibles,
Never used.
Meanwhile an old pitfall came to light.
When hadn't there been counterfeit
Emotions? But these now
Went undetected at the gala nights,
And "lumps of primal pain"
Were worn by daylight in resorts.
So much so, that many are preferring
To sit dry-eyed through the opera, to climb down

From the shabby rafters, having watched
Merely, and listened.
How beautiful these last performances
That fail to move us! Even as I write
They have broken ground for the new house
Whose boxes will be poured concrete emplacements,
Whose chandelier the roots of a huge tree.
On opening night
I shall be standing with others in the rain
As, one by one, skills, memories,
Prompter, electrician, negro star,
In street clothes, disappear
Through the unmarked stage door, rust-wreathed and
    massive.
Addio, one or two will say, *leb' wohl*,
And press my hand as if I, not they, were leaving.
Look for us. We have chosen—no—*You chose* ...
(The point will be to close
With their exact words—only by luck, however,
Reconstructable in dim suspense
Before the curtains part.)

MATINEES

for David Kalstone

A gray maidservant lets me in
To Mrs Livingston's box. It's already begun!
The box is full of grownups. She sits me down
Beside her. Meanwhile a ravishing din

Swells from below—Scene One
Of *Das Rheingold*. The entire proscenium
Is covered with a rippling azure scrim.
The three sopranos dart hither and yon

On invisible strings. Cold lights
Cling to bare arms, fair tresses. Flat
And natural aglitter like paillettes
Upon the great green sonorous depths float

Until with pulsing wealth the house is filled,
No one believing, everybody thrilled.

Lives of the Great Composers make it sound
Too much like cooking: "Sore beset,
He put his heart's blood into that quintet..."
So let us try the figure turned around

As in some Lives of Obscure Listeners:
"The strains of Cimarosa and Mozart
Flowed through his veins, and fed his solitary heart.
Long beyond adolescence [One infers

Your elimination, sweet Champagne
Drunk between acts!] the aria's remote
Control surviving his worst interval,

Tissue of sound and tissue of the brain
Would coalesce, and what the Masters wrote
Itself compose his features sharp and small."

Hilariously Dr Scherer took the guise
Of a bland smoothshaven Alberich whose ageold
Plan had been to fill my tooth with gold.
Another whiff of laughing gas,

And the understanding was implicit
That we must guard each other, this gold and I,
Against amalgamation by
The elemental pit.

Vague as to what dentist and tooth "stood for,"
One patient dreamer gathered something more.
A voice said in the speech of birds,

"My father having tampered with your mouth,
From now on, metal, music, myth
Will seem to taint its words."

We love the good, said Plato? He was wrong.
We love as well the wicked and the weak.
Flesh hugs its shaved plush. Twenty-four-hour-long
Galas fill the hulk of the Comique.

Flesh knows by now what dishes to avoid,
Tries not to brood on bomb or heart attack.
Anatomy is destiny, said Freud.
Soul is the brilliant hypochondriac.

Soul will cough blood and sing, and softer sing,
Drink poison, breathe her joyous last, a waltz
Rubato from his arms who sobs and stays

Behind, death after death, who fairly melts
Watching her turn from him, restored, to fling
Kisses into the furnace roaring praise.

The fallen cake, the risen price of meat,
Staircase run ten times up and down like scales
(Greek proverb: He who has no brain has feet)—
One's household opera never palls or fails.

The pipes' aubade. Recitatives.—Come back!
—I'm out of pills!—We'd love to!—What?—*Nothing*,
Let me be!—No, no, I'll drink it black...
The neighbors' chorus. The quick darkening

In which a prostrate figure must inquire
With every earmark of its being meant
Why God in Heaven harries him/her so.

The love scene (often cut). The potion. The tableau:
Sleepers folded in a magic fire,
Tongues flickering up from humdrum incident.

When Jan Kiepura sang His Handsomeness
Of Mantua those high airs light as lust
Attuned one's bare throat to the dagger-thrust.
Living for them would have been death no less.

Or Lehmann's Marschallin!—heartbreak so shrewd,
So ostrich-plumed, one ached to disengage
Oneself from a last love, at center stage,
To the beloved's dazzled gratitude.

What havoc certain Saturday afternoons
Wrought upon a bright young person's morals
I now leave to the public to condemn.

The point thereafter was to arrange for one's
Own chills and fever, passions and betrayals,
Chiefly in order to make song of them.

You and I, caro, seldom
Risk the real thing any more.
It's all too silly or too solemn.
Enough to know the score

From records or transcription
For our four hands. Old beauties, some
In advanced stages of decomposition,

Float up through the sustaining
Pedal's black and fluid medium.
Days like today

Even recur (wind whistling themes
From *Lulu*, and sun shining
On the rough Sound) when it seems
Kinder to remember than to play.

Dear Mrs Livingston,
I want to say that I am still in a daze
From yesterday afternoon.
I will treasure the experience always—

My very first Grand Opera! It was very
Thoughtful of you to invite
Me and am so sorry
That I was late, and for my coughing fit.

I play my record of the Overture
Over and over. I pretend
I am still sitting in the theatre.

I also wrote a poem which my Mother
Says I should copy out and send.
Ever gratefully, Your little friend...

POLA DIVA (AFTER AYOUB SINANO)

Sensational effects have subtle causes.
Whenever you sang Madame Butterfly
> At the Pera
> Opera
The crowd inhaled the garlic of your high
Flat C's, and therefore pelted you with roses.

Ah how your salad fragrances afloat
One fine day over doldrums canvas blue
> In the Pera
> Opera
Would merge with bosomy undulation to
Defray the steep expenses of each note.

Years later, in the dive where ends our tale,
You loll, mute queen (a lame divan for throne)
> Of the Pera
> Opera,
Whom evening's client, by your breath alone,
Knows to have been the Phanar's nightingale.

THE SUMMER PEOPLE

"... et l'hiver resterait la saison
intellectuelle créatrice."—Mallarmé

On our New England coast was once
A village white and neat
With Greek Revival houses,
Sailboats, a fishing fleet,

Two churches and two liquor stores,
An Inn, a Gourmet Shoppe,
A library, a pharmacy.
Trains passed but did not stop.

Gold Street was rich in neon,
Main Street in rustling trees
Untouched as yet by hurricanes
And the Dutch elm disease.

On Main the summer people
Took deep-rooted ease—
A leaf turned red, to town they'd head.
On Gold lived the Portuguese

Whose forebears had manned whalers.
Two years from the Azores
Saw you with ten gold dollars
Upon these fabled shores.

Feet still pace the whaler's deck
At the Caustic (Me.) Museum.
A small stuffed whale hangs overhead
As in the head a dream.

Slowly the fleet was shrinking.
The good-sized fish were few.
Town meetings closed and opened
With the question what to do.

55

Each year when manufacturers
Of chemicals and glues
Bid to pollute the harbor
It took longer to refuse.

Said Manuel the grocer,
"Vote for that factory,
And the summer people's houses
Will be up for sale, you'll see.

Our wives take in their laundry.
Our kids, they cut the grass
And baby-sit. The benefit
Comes home to all of us."

Someone else said, "Next winter
You'll miss that Chemical Plant."
Andrew breathed in Nora's ear:
"Go, grasshopper! Go, ant!"

These two were summer neighbors.
They loved without desire.
Both, now pushing fifty,
Had elsewhere played with fire.

Of all the summer people
Who dwelt in pigeonholes,
Old Navy or Young Married,
The Bad Sports, the Good Souls,

These were the Amusing,
The Unconventional ones—
Plus Andrew's Jane (she used a cane
And shook it at his puns)

And Nora's mother Margaret
With her dawn-colored hair,
Her novels laid in Europe
That she wrote in a garden chair.

"Where's Andrew?" Margaret queried
As Nora entered the room.
"Didn't he want to come over?
It seems to be my doom

To spend long lonely evenings.
Don't we *know* anyone?"
"Dozens of people, Mother."
"But none of them are fun!

The summer already seems endless
And it's only the first of July.
My eyes are too weak for reading
And I am too strong to cry.

I wish I weren't a widow,
I wish you weren't divorced—
Oh, by the way, I heard today
About a man named Frost

Who's bought the Baptist church
And means to do it over."
"Mother, he sounds like just the type
I don't need for a lover."

Andrew at the piano
Let the ice in his nightcap melt.
Mendelssohn's augmentations
Were very deeply felt.

Jane cleaned her paintbrushes
With fingers rheumatic and slow.
Their son came back from the movies,
She called a vague hello

But he'd bounded upstairs already,
Jarring three petals loose
From today's bunch of roses
Not dry yet—pink, cream, puce.

A young man spoke to Margaret
At a party: "Don't be bored.
I've read your books, I like your looks"—
Then vanished in the horde.

Her hostess said when questioned,
"Why, that's Interesting Jack Frost.
He's fixing up that eyesore
With no regard for cost.

Don't ask me where he comes from
Or why he settled here.
He's certainly attractive,
To judge by the veneer."

One thing led to another,
And long before summer's end,
Margaret, Nora, Andrew, Jane
Had found them a new friend.

Jack Frost was years older
Than his twenty-year-old face.
He loved four-hand piano
And gladly took the bass,

Loved also bridge but did not play
So well as to offend,
Loved to gossip, loved croquet,
His money loved to spend

On food and drink and flowers,
Loved entertaining most.
The happy few who'd been there knew
Him as a famous host.

The church was now a folly
Cloud-white and palest blue—
Lanterns, stained glass, mirrors,
Polar bear rugs, bamboo,

Armchairs of gleaming buffalo-horn,
The titter of wind chimes,
A white cat, a blue cushion
Stitched with the cat's name, Grimes.

"Proud Grimes, proud loyal kitty,"
Jack said, "I love you best."
Two golden eyes were trimmed to slits,
Gorgeously unimpressed.

Ken the Japanese "houseboy"
(Though silver-haired and frail)
Served many a curious hot hors-d'oeuvre
And icy cold cocktail.

The new friends, that first evening,
Sat on till half past two.
"This man," said Andrew on the street,
"Is too good to be true.

One views with faint misgivings
The bounty of the young."
"Speak for yourself," said Nora
Or the Cointreau on her tongue.

"Well, *I* think he's enchanting,"
Said Margaret, "and what's more
In the long run he'll find, for fun,
No one to match us four."

October came too quickly,
The leaves turned red and sere,
Time for the summer people
To pack up and call it a year.

In the mind's mouth summers later
Ken's farewell banquet melts.
Where would Jack spend the winter?
Why, here of course—where else?

"Stay here all winter? Really,
The things some people do!"
"Whither thou goest, Margaret,
To thee I will be true."

"Come see us in the city."
"My lovely Nora, no.
Too full of dull, dull people
And dirty, dirty snow."

"Come see *us* in Barbados."
"Forgive me, dearest Jane.
I've planned a Northern winter."
So they cajoled in vain.

The next days Jack lay drowsing,
Grimes in the bend of his knees.
He woke one dusk to eat a rusk
And smile at the bare trees.

The first huge flakes descended
Hexagonal, unique.
The panes put forth white leafage.
The harbor froze in a week.

The shrieking children skated
Upon its harsh white jewel,
Whose parents stayed indoors and paid
Outrageous bills for fuel.

Great lengths of gnarled crystal
Glittered from porch and eave.
It was, in short, a winter
You had to see to believe.

Whole nights, a tower window
Threw light upon the storm.
"Jack's sure artistic," Manuel said,
"But how does he keep warm?"

Ken climbed the stair one March dusk.
"Dear Jack-san, now am ord,
Dream of my Kyushu virrage
Where nobody catch cord."

"Together, Ken, we'll go there,
But for the moment stay.
What would I do without you?"
Ken bowed and turned away.

Jack stood up. The cat scuttled
Discreetly out of sight.
Jack's eyes were wet. Pride and regret
Burned in his heart all night.

A mild sun rose next morning.
The roofs began to steam
Where snow had melted. Winter
Was ending like a dream.

Alerted and elated
The summer friends came back.
Their exile had been tiresome,
Each now confessed to Jack.

His garden made them welcome;
Ken had spent May on his knees
Among the plots. From Chinese pots
On the church porch small trees

Rose thick with purple blossoms
Pendulous as Turks.
Said Andrew gravely, "I have seen
The fuchsia, and it works."

That summer was the model
For several in a row—
High-water marks of humor
And humankindness, no

Discord at cards, at picnics,
Charades or musicales.
Their faces bright with pleasure might
Not have displeased Frans Hals.

Jane, speaking of pictures,
Had started one of Grimes
Drugged on Jack's lap. Those sessions
Made for the merriest times.

Margaret brought out her gripping
Stories of love and war,
Peking and Nice. They held their peace
Who'd heard them told before.

Nora, one August afternoon,
Burst in with currant fool
Enough for the whole village.
Its last sweet molecule

Eaten, they blushed like truants.
"Shame on us every one,"
Jane sighed, "we've got no fiber."
And Margaret: "Oh, the fun!

Let's stay for Christmas. Andrew,
You can play Santa Claus!"
Jack gave a cry. Into his thigh
The cat had dug its claws.

Jane's canvas, scarred and peeling
Turned up at the village fair
The other day. I'm sad to say
It found a customer.

The Chemical Plant director
Bought it for his wife
To overpaint with symbols
Flat as her palette knife.

They're a perfectly nice couple
So long as you steer clear
Of art and politics and such—
But to resume. That year

Jack's friends did stay for Christmas,
The next year into Lent,
A third year stayed all winter
To their own astonishment.

Logs burned, the sparks flew upward.
The whiteness when they woke
Struck them as of a genius
Positively baroque,

Invention's breast and plumage,
Flights of the midnight Swan...
The facts are in Margaret's journal
To be published when she's gone.

I should perhaps have trusted
To dry-eyed prose like hers.
The meter grows misleading,
Given my characters.

For figures in a ballad
Lend themselves to acts
Passionate and simple.
A bride weeps. A tree cracks.

A young king, an old outlaw
Whose temperament inclines
To strife where breakers thunder
Bleeds between the lines.

But I have no such hero,
No fearful deeds—unless
We count their quiet performance
By Time or Tenderness.

These two are the past masters
Of rime, tone, overtone.
They write upon our faces
Until the pen strikes bone.

Time passes softly, scarcely
Felt by me or you.
And then, at an odd moment,
Tenderness passes, too.

That January midday
Jack's head fell to his knee.
Margaret stopped in mid-sentence—
Whatever could it be?

"He's sound asleep," said Nora.
"So clever of him. If
Only I were! Your stories
Bore everybody stiff."

"What can she mean," said Margaret,
"Speaking to me like that?"
"I mean you're gaga, Mother."
"And you, my child, are fat."

Jack murmured in his slumber,
"I didn't sleep a wink
All during last night's blizzard.
Where am I? Where's my drink?"

His eyes flew wide. "I'm sorry,
I'm sick, I have to go."
He took his coat and tottered
Out into windless snow.

The dogwood at the corner,
Unbending in a burst
Of diamond levity, let drop:
Old friend, think! First things first,

Not June in January—
"Be still!" cried Jack, and bit
His stupid tongue. A snowflake stung
Silence back into it.

Ken helped him up the tower stair,
"Rie down, Jack-san, now rest."
He fell among white blankets,
Grimes heavy on his chest.

Margaret went round next morning
And rang. No one replied.
She found Ken sleeping on the stair,
A wineglass at his side.

A white blur sped to meet her—
Was it that ghastly cat?
Grimes spat, crouched, sprang and sank a fang
Into her, just like that!

She screamed. A stern young doctor,
Summoned out of the void,
Dressed her wound, then telephoned
To have the cat destroyed.

Jack flew to the Police Chief,
Called the SPCA,
Despairing thought that Margaret
Herself might save the day.

She kept him standing, coldly
Displayed her bandaged calf.
He spoiled it all by failing
To check a thoughtless laugh.

Two men with gloves were waiting.
They caught Grimes in a sack.
Two good whiffs of ether
And his gold eyes shut on Jack.

That same night, Grimes in ermine
And coronet of ice
Called him by name, cried vengeance,
Twitching his long tail twice.

Jack woke in pitch dark, burning,
Freezing, leapt dry-lipped
From bed, threw clothes on, neither
Packed nor reflected, slipped

Money between pages
Of Ken's dog-eared almanac,
Then on the sleeping village
Forever turned his back.

He must have let a month go by
Before he sent them all
Postcards of some Higher Thing—
The Jungfrau, white and tall.

"Well, that answers our question,"
Said Margaret looking grim.
They dealt with Jack from then on
By never mentioning him.

Languid as convalescents,
Dreading the color green,
They braced themselves for summer's
Inexorable routine.

Andrew at the piano,
Six highballs gone or more,
Played Brahms, his "venerable beads"
Fixed on the flickering score.

Kneeling in her muggy
Boxwood garden Jane
Stopped weeding, tried to rise
But could not move for pain.

She saw her son's tanned fingers
Lowering the blind
Of an attic window.
She did not know his mind.

Croquet and hectic banter
From Margaret's back yard
Broke upon her twinges.
"*En*," shrieked Nora, "*garde!*"

"Oh God, this life's so pointless,
So wearing," Margaret said.
"You're telling me," Andrew agreed.
"High time we both were dead."

"It *is*. I have pills—let's take them!"
He looked at her with wit.
"Just try. You know we'd never
Hear the end of it."

Their laughter floated on the dusk.
Ken thought of dropping in,
But his nails were cracked and dirty
And his breath smelled of gin.

"Missed you at Town Meeting
Last night," said Manuel
As Nora fingered honeydews.
"Things didn't go too well.

Fact is, the Plant got voted in.
I call it a downright
Pity you summer people
Didn't care enough to fight."

"Manuel, there have been winters
We stayed here," Nora said.
"That makes us year-round people."
The grocer scratched his head.

"I guess I don't mean season
So much as a point of view."
It made her mad. She'd meant to add,
"And we do care, we *do*,"

But it was too late, she didn't,
Didn't care one bit.
Manuel counted out her change:
"...*and* ten. Will that be it?"

"Insufferable rudeness!
Of course by now it's clear,"
Said Margaret, laying down her trumps,
"We must all get out of here."

"We go next week," admitted
Jane with a guilty air.
"Old friends in Locust Valley
Keep asking us down there."

"Besides," said Andrew quickly,
"This climate's bothersome.
I may take Jane to Port-of-Spain—
All *my* roads lead to rum."

"So they do. Well, that's lovely,
Leaving us in the lurch,"
Said Nora, "just like what's-his-name
Who had the Baptist church."

"The summer's over," said Margaret.
"But you misunderstood:
I meant this town was ruined.
We must all get out for good."

Ken wrapped some Canton saucers
Like a conspirator,
To be exchanged for credit
At the corner liquor store.

September. Dismal rainstorms
Made everything a blur,
Lashed Margaret into action—
City life for her!

"I'll stay up here," said Nora,
"A month or two. I need
Time to think things over,
Listen to records, read."

She drove home from Caustic
Where Margaret caught her plane.
The windshield streamed in silence,
The wipers thrashed in vain.

October. Early twilights.
To the wharf came a blue
And silver haul of fish too small
For anything but glue.

The boatyard was a boneyard,
Bleached hull, moon-eaten chain.
The empty depot trembled
At the scream of a passing train.

Nora long past midnight
Lay rereading *Emma*,
Unmoved for once by a daughter's
Soon-to-be-solved dilemma.

And late dawns. The first victim
Of Main Street's seventeen
Doomed elms awoke and feebly shook
Its sparrow-tambourine.

In the November mildness
Rose delicate green spears—
Spring flowers Ken had planted.
His small eyes filled with tears:

They were coming up too early!
He sniffed and went indoors.
He dusted all the objects,
Polished the bare floors,

Bathed and oiled his person;
Now put on his best clothes,
Thought up a huge sweet cocktail,
And sipping at it chose

The first words of a letter
He had long meant to write.
But wait, his glass was empty—
A foolish oversight.

Nora heard him coughing.
She stopped her evening stroll
And went to see. With courtesy
Both sinister and droll

Ken bowed low, made her welcome,
Concocted a new drink.
Darkly hilarious he said,
"Rong rife!" and gave a wink.

One didn't need to be Nora
To see that things weren't right.
In his brown silk kimono
Ken sat there high as a kite.

His talk was incoherent:
Jack—his mother's loom—
The weather—his green island—
Flowers he'd not see bloom—

The dead cat—a masked actor—
Ghosts up in the hills . . .
And then those frightful spasms
Followed by small white pills.

Nora thought food might help him
And ran back for a cup
Of homemade soup. He took a sip,
Set down the cup, got up:

"Dear Missy-san, too sorty.
Night-night now. Kissing hand."
This done, Ken headed for the stair,
Though hardly able to stand.

Next day she found him lying
Cold on his bed. "I knew,
I *knew!*" sobbed Nora over the phone.
"But what was there to do?

He wasn't kin or even friend,
Just old and sick, poor dear.
It was his right to take his life,
Not mine to interfere."

"Exactly," said her mother.
"I'll come tomorrow. Jack?
Try the address on Ken's letter.
A wire may bring him back."

It did not. The two ladies
Arranged the funeral,
Then sat at home in silence
Deeper than I can tell.

Jack sent a check weeks later
And wrote them from Tibet
A long sad charming letter,
But friendship's sun had set.

December. "I think sometimes,"
Said Margaret dreamily,
"That Jack was a delusion
Of the whole community.

No reasonable adult
Starts acting like a child.
How else can you explain it?
He had us all beguiled."

Nora looked up. The mirror
Struck her a glancing blow.
Her hair once blonde as summer
Was dull and streaked with snow.

"Oh tell me, Mother, tell me
Where do the years go?
I'm old, my life is ending!"
"Baby, I know, I know."

As soon as they were calmer,
"I also," Margaret said,
"Know what to do about it.
So get up from that bed.

I know a clever fairy
Who puts gold back in hair.
I know of jets to Rio.
It will be summer there."

Come May, Ken's garden blossomed
In memory of him—
Hyacinth, narcissus
White as seraphim.

Jane and Andrew saw it.
They'd driven up to sell
Their house at a tidy profit
To the Head of Personnel.

It had grown so big, so empty.
Their lawn was choked with weeds,
Their son in California
Barefoot, all beard and beads.

They stood among Ken's flowers
Gazing without a word.
Jane put her hand in Andrew's.
The cat in heaven purred.

And then a faint piano
Sounded—from where? They tried
The door, it floated open,
Inviting them inside.

Sitting at the keyboard
In a cloud of brilliant notes
A boy they'd both seen somewhere
Was playing random notes.

He rose as if uncertain
Whether to speak or run.
Jane said, "I know who you are,
You're Joey, Manuel's son,

Who used to cut the grass for us.
Look at you, grown so tall!"
He grinned. "I won a scholarship
At M.I.T. this fall

To study cybernetics
And flute—it's worth a try.
I used to come and talk to Ken.
I miss that little guy."

"One by one, like swallows . . ."
Said Andrew in the gloom
That fell when Joe departed.
"Dear God, look at this room."

Full ashtrays, soft-drink bottles
Told an artless tale
Of adolescent revels.
Tan stacks of ninth-class mail

Lay tumbled helter-skelter.
A chill in the stirred air
Sent Jane outdoors and Andrew
To brave the tower stair.

Moon after moon had faded
The papers on Jack's desk:
Unfinished calculation,
Doodle and arabesque.

One window framed the sunset
Transfiguring Main Street,
Its houses faintly crimson
But upright in defeat.

The other faced the harbor.
Lights of the Chemical Plant
Gloated over water.
"The grasshopper, the ant,"

Breathed Andrew, recollecting
His long ago remark,
Then shut both views behind him
And felt his way down in dark.

JAMES MERRILL

James Merrill was born in New York City and now lives in Stonington, Connecticut. He is the author of four earlier books of poems: *Nights and Days* (National Book Award in Poetry for 1967), *Water Street* (1962), *The Country of a Thousand Years of Peace* (1959), and *First Poems* (1951); two novels: *The (Diblos) Notebook* (1965), and *The Seraglio* (1957); and two plays: *The Immortal Husband* (first produced in 1955 and published in PLAYBOOK the following year) and, in one act, *The Bait*, published in ARTIST'S THEATRE (1960).